HAPPY EVER CRAFTER

DINOSAURS

ANNALEES LIM

WAYLAND
www.waylandbooks.co.uk

First published in Great Britain in 2018 by Wayland
Copyright © Hodder and Stoughton 2018

Senior Commissioning Editor: Melanie Palmer
Design: Square and Circus
Illustrations: Supriya Sahai

Additional illustrations: Freepik

HB ISBN 978 1 5263 0757 6
PB ISBN 978 1 5263 0758 3

FSC
www.fsc.org
MIX
Paper from
responsible sources
FSC® C104740

Printed in China

Wayland
An imprint of
Hachette Children's Group
Part of Hodder and Stoughton
Carmelite House
50 Victoria Embankment
London EC4Y 0DZ

An Hachette UK Company
www.hachette.co.uk

SAFETY INFORMATION:
Please ask an adult for help with any activities
that could be tricky, involve cooking or handling
glass. Ask adult permission when appropriate.

Due care has been taken to ensure the activities
are safe and the publishers regret they cannot
accept liability for any loss or injuries sustained.

CONTENTS

Dinosaurs

For millions of years dinosaurs ruled the Earth. They lived on every continent, in different terrains and climates, constantly evolving to suit their changing environments.

The word dinosaur comes from the Greek word for 'terrible lizard' but this does not mean that all dinosaurs were big and scary. While a lot of sharp-clawed dinosaurs were carnivores (meat-eaters) there were many more who were herbivores (plant-eaters). You can tell which ones these were by looking out for their blunt hooves or scale-like toenails.

FACT!

Did you know that some scientists believe that lots of dinosaurs had feathers, including the Tyrannosaurus Rex. The closest living relative to the dinosaur is the chicken!

A paleontologist is a person who finds and studies fossils to learn more about dinosaurs and how they lived. When you see dinosaur skeletons in museums you aren't actually looking at real bones, they're fossils. This special type of rock replaces the buried bones, making an exact replica in its place.

TOP TIP

With this book you can make lots of discoveries yourself and learn more about dinosaurs, too. Make fun and simple crafts using lots of materials you will find around your house, then dress up in costumes and plan the best dino-disco party in town. All of these projects are easy to follow but remember to always ask an adult to help you before you get started!

No one really knows what dinosaurs looked like as we only have their bones to study. When using this book use your imagination to create the most unique-looking dinosaurs. Use lots of different colours and even try adding feathers to your creations!

BIG BEASTS FANCY DRESS

Recycle old pieces of clothing and transform them into dinosaur costumes. These prehistoric projects are easy to make but you can add your own designs, too. Try mixing different materials together, changing colours or combining projects to create a brand new dinosaur.

SPINOSAURUS SPINE

A Spinosaurus is one of the largest and longest dinosaurs ever to roam the Earth. These carnivores had a long face with a large bone fin on their back called a sail. They lived both on the land and in the sea, just like crocodiles do, and mainly had a diet of fish.

YOU WILL NEED:

- LARGE CARDBOARD BOX • SCISSORS
- PENCIL • THICK CARD • PAINT
- THIN CARD • GLUE STICK
- PAINTBRUSH • RIBBON/STRING

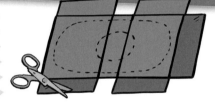

1. Flatten out a large cardboard box and cut it into a long oval shape with a hole in the middle.

2. Make 4 small holes on the edges of the oval shape.

4. Stick 'L' shaped card to either side of the circle sail.

3. Cut out a half circle sail and a triangle tail shape. Stick these to one half of the oval.

5. Paint the whole thing and leave to dry before threading ribbon or string through the holes.

TRICERATOPS HEADDRESS

A Triceratops is a large four-legged dinosaur with a frill made from bone around its head. Its name means 'three-horned face' because it has one on its nose and two at the top of its head. The horns were used for defence rather than hunting as they liked to eat low-lying plants.

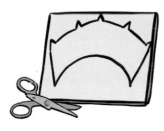

1. Cut out a crescent shape from some scrap card, making sure you have 5 small triangle shapes on top, too.

2. Bend this over the top of the hat at an angle and staple it in place at the sides.

YOU WILL NEED:
- AN OLD BASEBALL CAP
- CARD • SCISSORS • STICKY TAPE
- STAPLER • NEWSPAPER • GREEN /BLACK/WHITE TISSUE PAPER
- WHITE CRAFT GLUE

3. Scrunch up bits of newspaper and stick them on to the hat to add details to the frill and make eyes and a nose.

4. Make three cones from circles of card and tape them on to the peak of the cap in a triangle formation.

5. Cover the whole thing with layers of green, black and white tissue paper and white craft glue. Leave to dry in a warm place before wearing.

EUOPLOCEPHALUS TAIL

The Euoplocephalus was a herbivore and had large plates covering its body like armour. It had spikes all over its body and head and would swing its long tail, with a boulder-shaped hammer at the end, to defend itself from predators.

YOU WILL NEED:

- AN OLD PAIR OF TROUSERS
- NEEDLE AND THREAD • NEWSPAPER
- ELASTIC BANDS • PAPER • SCISSORS
- WHITE CRAFT GLUE

1. Cut the waist band off some trousers and separate the legs.

2. Sew one of the legs on to the waistband and stuff with scrunched up newspaper.

3. Put the other trouser leg inside to make a long tail and secure it with an elastic band.

4. Stuff the top section of the second trouser leg with more stuffing and hold in place with and elastic band. Cut off the excess trouser leg.

5. Decorate the tail with paper spikes, stuck on with glue.

PTERODACTYLUS WINGS

People often mistakenly call all winged reptiles Pterodactyls, but the word for this group of creatures is Pterosaurs. One of the most recognised members of the group is the Pterodactylus. Its name means 'winged finger' as it has stretched, bat-like wings.

YOU WILL NEED:

- LONG SLEEVED T-SHIRT • SCISSORS
- FABRIC GLUE • NEEDLE AND THREAD • PAPER • FABRIC PAINT OR FELT-TIP PENS

1. Cut the body section off the long sleeved t-shirt.

2. Open out the fabric and cut diagonally so that it makes two triangles.

3. Glue or stitch the fabric triangles on to each sleeve. Make two paper feet and stick them to the bottom of the wings.

4. Paint your costume using fabric paints or felt-tip pens.

What do you call a dinosaur who knows lots of words?
A Thesaurus

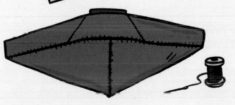

9

PREHISTORIC PARTY PLANNING

The best birthday bashes and holiday celebrations don't organise themselves. They can take weeks of planning but it will be all worth it to see your excited guests enjoying themselves. Follow these top tips and handy reminders to help you plan an epic Jurassic-themed party.

KEEP A LIST

Write down everything you will need to do for the party. Give yourself plenty of time to prepare, especially if you have big plans to decorate, bake and build. Mark your 'to do' list with a dinosaur sticker or draw a big dino footprint alongside each task to show when you've done it.

1. Land of the dinosaurs: Transport your guests back in time millions of years by creating the perfect dino habitat. There are plenty of ideas on page 16 to transform your party space.

2. Dino dress up: If your party has a theme, you might want to ask your guests to wear fancy dress, too. Find some costume projects on page 6 for inspiration. You can always make extras and put them in box so people can try them on.

3. Play some games: Roaring and stomping around like dinosaurs can be great fun, especially when you're playing fun games. The projects on page 12 all have a dino theme and can be made by yourself beforehand or as a fun party activity for you to entertain your guests with.

4. Ferocious food: Make sure you have plenty of food ready to feed your monstrous gang. Turn to page 20 for simple recipes to stop any stomachs from roaring and rumbling.

5. Monster makes: On page 24 you will find lots of mini makes which are perfect to add to your decorations, give out as thank you gifts or to award as prizes for the best dressed dinosaurs at the party.

INVITATIONS

One of the most important things to remember is the invitations. Send one to everyone you want to invite and make sure you tell them all the information they need. Use this dinosaur themed invitation as a template to make your own.

What: Let everyone know why you are celebrating.

To: Invite your best prehistoric pals to the party.

You are invited to my BIRTHDAY PARTY...

To: _____

Where: _____

When: _____

Dress code: _____

RSVP: _____

When and Where: Write the date, address and time of the party.

Dress code: What would you like everyone to wear?

RSVP: Ask people to let you know if they can come.

PARTY GAMES

These four party projects are all made from things you will find around the house. By recycling and reusing things, you are saving money and being environmentally friendly. You can ask friends or neighbours if they have any of the things you need, too.

THE BIG DIG

Paleontologists study dinosaurs by looking at their fossils. There are lots of places all around the world where you can look for fossilised bones and new types of dinosaurs. You have to be very careful when you excavate not to damage the bones, by using lots of tools like shovels and brushes.

YOU WILL NEED:

- TIN FOIL • KITCHEN TOWEL
- WHITE CRAFT GLUE • PAPER
- COLOURED FELT-TIP PENS

1. Mould the tin foil into bone shapes. You will need 5 for each person playing the game.

2. Cover each bone with a layer of kitchen towel and craft glue. Leave to dry.

3. Draw a coloured spot on each bone with the felt-tip pens. Each set of bones should be a different colour.

4. Draw a dinosaur shape on a piece of paper. Make one for each player.

HOW TO PLAY

Scatter the bones into the bottom of a large container or paddling pool and cover with a layer of sand. Decide who is going to collect which colour then place the dino sheet on the floor. At the start, everyone runs towards the dig and uses their paintbrush to brush off the sand and reveal the bones. Once you have found your colour of bone, run back to the start and place the bone on the sheet. Then run back to find another bone. The winner is the person who finds all 5 of their bones the fastest.

DINO HUNT

YOU WILL NEED:

- KITCHEN ROLL TUBE • PAPER
- SCISSORS • STICKY TAPE
- STRING • COLOURED CARD
- DRY WIPE MARKER

Did you know that different dinosaurs lived at different periods of time called Triassic, Jurassic and Cretaceous? This means that you would never find some of the dinosaurs you've heard of living alongside each other. A Tyrannosaurus Rex would never have met a Stegosaurus and an Iguanodon would never have seen a Triceratops.

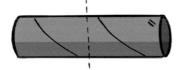

1. Cut the kitchen roll tube in half and cover each with some paper.

2. Stick the two tubes together with sticky tape

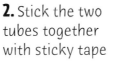

3. Stick some string to the sides of the tube to make the binoculars. Make one pair for each player.

4. Cut out coloured dinosaur shapes from the card and stick some tape on to one side.

5. Stick a loop of string to each one.

HOW TO PLAY

Write a letter on each dinosaur, on the shiny side, so that it spells a word. Hang up the letters in a tree or on the branches of a bush. Players who do not know what the word is use their binoculars to find the letters. The first person to unscramble the letters and shout out the correct word wins! You can wipe off the letters and write on news ones to play another game.

T-REX RAMPAGE

The Tyrannosaurus Rex was a large and powerful carnivore that had a very large head, small arms and a long tail to help it balance. Most lived in North America and evidence of their existence was first found in 1874 in Colorado, USA. But it wasn't until 1900 that the first nearly complete skeleton was discovered and then officially named two years later.

YOU WILL NEED:

- THIN CARDBOARD • STAPLER
- WHITE PAPER • FELT-TIP PENS
- SCRAP FABRIC

1. Make a cardboard circle that fits around your head.

2. Staple two more strips of paper to the front.

3. Glue some white triangle teeth on to the strips of paper.

4. Draw on some eyes with a felt-tip pen.

5. Cut out a triangle shape from some fabric. This will be the tail. Make a T-Rex set for each player.

HOW TO PLAY

Everyone wears their own headdress and tucks in the triangle tail into the back of their waistband. Tuck arms into your t-shirt so only your hands are visible. When the game starts, everyone needs to try and grab the tails from the backs of the other players. If your tail is taken, you are out. The winner is the last person to have their tail still tucked in.

FEED THE DINOSAUR

Paleontologists can tell a lot about how a dinosaur lived by what sort of teeth they had. Some had rows and rows of sharp teeth, and some had smaller, flatter teeth. This showed whether they ate mostly meat or plants.

YOU WILL NEED:
- LARGE CARDBOARD BOXES
- GLUE STICK • WHITE PAPER
- SCISSORS • PAINT • PAINTBRUSH
- NEWSPAPER

1. Cut a hole from the front of the box.

2. Stick white triangles inside the hole.

3. Decorate the box with more card to make head, eyes, nose and horns.

4. Paint the box in different colours and leave to dry.

5. Scrunch up pieces of paper or newspaper and put in a pile.

HOW TO PLAY
See how many balls of newspaper you can throw into the dinosaur's mouth in 60 seconds. Take turns and keep your scores written down to see who is the ultimate winner.

PARTY DECORATIONS

Decorating a room can be a fun, quick and simple way to set a scene and get everyone in the party mood. Hang things from the ceiling, cover tables and chairs and even replace paintings and photographs with your own hangings – just be sure to ask an adult first!

IN THE JUNGLE

In the age of the dinosaurs, there were no buildings or roads so the landscape looked very different to today. During the Jurassic period the weather was often wet and warm, which was an ideal environment for lots of green plants to grow amongst the tall trees.

1. Paint a green wash over sheets of newspaper and leave to dry.

2. Fold a sheet in half and draw on half a fern shape. Cut the shapes out.

YOU WILL NEED:

- WATERED-DOWN GREEN PAINT
- NEWSPAPER
- PENCIL • PAINTBRUSH
- STRING • SCISSORS
- STICKY TAPE

3. Gather the fern leaves together in a bunch around a length of string.

4. Wrap the sticky tape around the bunch and hang up.

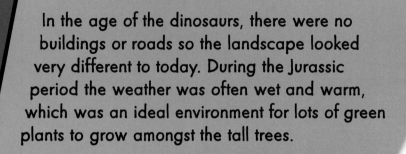

BARYONYX BONES

Baryonyx means 'heavy claw' so called as it has a very large claw on each thumb. It was first discovered in a clay pit in 1983 in Surrey, England and the original fossil can still be seen at the Natural History Museum, London.

1. Cut out two claw shapes from some thin card.

Where did the T-Rex go to get his shopping?
The Dino-Store

2. Tape these on to the edges of a small yoghurt pot.

3. Use more masking tape to join the sides of the claw together.

4. Rub the surface lightly with a brown crayon. Colour the base a darker brown by pressing harder with the same crayon.

17

TYRANNOTITAN TEETH

The skeleton of a Tyrannotitan was only discovered in 2005 in a farm in Argentina, South America. It was a fierce carnivore that had about 60 teeth in its giant jaw and was one of the main predators of its time.

YOU WILL NEED:

- LIGHTWEIGHT PAPER
- TWO BALLOONS • STICKY TAPE
- PAPER • SCISSORS

1. Blow up two balloons, one slightly bigger than the other.

2. Stick one on to the other with sticky tape.

3. Make some paper arms, legs and tail. Cut out and stick on to the balloon.

4. Cut out triangles from some black paper. Discard the triangles and keep the leftover piece of paper.

TOP TIP

If you rub the balloon on to your jumper, the static electricity will stick it to the ceiling.

5. Stick this paper on to the balloon and add eyes, too.

TROODON EGGS

A Troodon is one of the smaller dinosaurs, measuring up to just 90 cm in height. It laid around 20 eggs over a period of about a week in small clusters on the ground. It is thought that the eggs were looked after and kept warm by the adult sitting on them rather than being buried in the ground.

YOU WILL NEED:
- TWO WATER BOTTLES WITH ROUNDED BOTTOMS • POLYSTYRENE
- WHITE CRAFT GLUE • KITCHEN TOWEL • STICKY TAPE

1. Cut two water bottles in half.

2. Tape the two bottom halves together using sticky tape.

3. Break in some chunks of polystyrene and mix in some glue.

4. Paint the textured glue around the bottles and leave to dry.

5. Tear the kitchen roll in pieces and stick a layer on top of the bottle using the white craft glue.

TOP TIP
Use these as decorations for the table. Write your guests' names on them so they know where to sit. Or scatter them in the middle to make a centrepiece.

19

PARTY FOOD

Dinosaurs were thought to have swallowed large rocks to help things digest better in their stomach but you won't need any stones to help your guests enjoy these recipes! Remember to wash your hands before cooking and always ask an adult for help using the oven or sharp knives.

DINO NESTS

It is hard to find fossilised nests so it's unknown what materials were used and how they were built. But as scientists learn more about the link between dinosaurs and birds, it is becoming more likely that lots of species of dinosaurs used open nests on the floor to look after their young.

YOU WILL NEED:
- WHEAT CEREAL • MILK CHOCOLATE
- DARK CHOCOLATE DROPS
- DRIED CHERRIES • PAPER BOWL
- CLING FILM

1. Break up some wheat cereal into a bowl.

2. Melt a milk chocolate bar and pour in to the cereal. Add some dark chocolate drops and dried cherries into the mixture and mix well.

TOP TIP
Add chocolate eggs to the nest to complete. You could always add some jelly reptiles too, to look like some have just hatched.

4. Line a paper bowl with cling film.

5. Spoon the mixture into the bowl and press into the sides to make a nest shape. Leave to cool before removing from the bowl.

ICE AGE MERINGUES

Ice Ages have been happening from time to time over the course of the Earth's history. There have been five major Ice Ages where the Earth's temperature lowers and the polar ice caps grow larger, covering more of the planet in ice and glaciers. Did you know that we are actually in an Ice Age right now? It is in the warmer period and this could still last for millions of years!

YOU WILL NEED:

- MERINGUE NESTS
- VANILLA ICE CREAM • LEMON CURD
- COCONUT

1. Crush up some meringue nests in a bowl.

2. Slightly soften the vanilla ice cream and add to the meringues. Mix well.

4. Add a scoop of the ice cream mixture on top of the nests.

3. Spread a spoonful of lemon curd on top of a meringue nest.

5. Sprinkle some coconut on top.

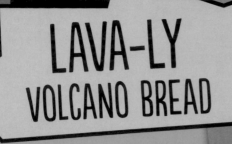

LAVA-LY VOLCANO BREAD

YOU WILL NEED:

- OVENPROOF BOWL • RAMEKIN
- BAKING TRAY • GREASEPROOF PAPER • PIZZA DOUGH • GRATED CHEESE • TOMATO SALSA

Volcanoes are usually formed in mountains. They act like a vent so the magma and gas that's built up underneath the Earth's surface can escape. There are many all over the planet. Most are 'extinct' meaning they will not erupt. Some are 'dormant' which means they could erupt in the future. Others are 'active' so you are likely to see lava flowing out of them one day.

1. Place an oven proof bowl and ramekin on to a baking tray.

2. Cover this with a sheet of greaseproof paper, making sure you make a dip at the top.

3. Roll out the pizza dough and lie on top of the greaseproof paper and sprinkle with cheese.

BAKE!

5. Serve with a tomato salsa dip in the top.

4. Bake as per the pizza dough instructions, or until golden brown.

MARSHMALLOW MEGALOSAURUS

The Megalosaurus was a large two-legged dinosaur with two short arms and three sharp claws on each hand. When it was first discovered people thought it was a part of an old elephant, as no one knew about dinosaurs then.

YOU WILL NEED:

- CRUSHED CHOCOLATE BISCUITS
- BAKING TRAY • SMALL AND LARGE MARSHMALLOWS • DARK CHOCOLATE
- ICING PENS

1. Fill a baking tray with crushed chocolate biscuits.

2. Melt some dark chocolate – this will act like your glue.

3. Make the head and hips from 3 large marshmallows. Place them into the crushed biscuits.

4. 'Draw' with the mini marshmallows to make the spine, tail, ribs, arms and legs. Join it all together by pouring in the melted chocolate.

5. Use an icing pen to add more details to the head and claws.

CRAFT-O-SAURUS

Gather together all your craft materials and start making. These projects will all fit in well with your other party preparations, or you can just make them for fun. Cover surfaces before you start to stop things getting messy, and remember to tidy up afterwards.

PLATEOSAURUS PLATES

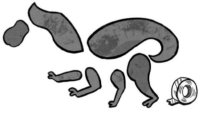

The Plateosaurus is one of the earliest dinosaurs to have roamed the Earth. It was a two-legged plant eater that had a long neck with a small head, and its name means 'flat lizard'. Lots of fossils of this dinosaur have been discovered and scientists believe that they used to live in herds.

YOU WILL NEED:

- PAPER PLATE • GREEN PAINTS
- PAINTBRUSH OR SPONGE • PENCIL
- SCISSORS • STICKY TAPE
- FELT-TIP PENS

1. Paint a paper plate in different shades of green. Try using a sponge to add some texture.

2. Draw a body, head, tail, arms and legs in parts on to the plate.

3. Cut them out and arrange in the right order.

4. Stick them together by overlapping the edges and taping the back.

5. Draw on details to the face and markings to the body.

CARNOTAURUS

A Carnotaurus' name means 'meat-eating bull' and it is thought to be one of the fastest of its kind. It had a very textured and bumpy body, and would use the two horns on the side of its head to hunt, defend and fight. Its arms were so small that they would not had been much use at all.

YOU WILL NEED:

- TWO SHEETS OF SANDPAPER
- COLOURED CRAYONS • GLUE STICK
- BLUE PIECE OF PAPER

1. Colour one sheet of sandpaper using a green crayon.

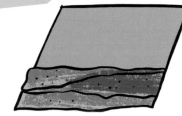

2. Tear up half the green into strips and stick it on to the bottom of a blue piece of paper to make a landscape.

3. Tear the other half of the green sheet into leaf shapes and stick them around the edge.

4. Draw the Carnotaurus on to another piece of sandpaper using more crayons and roughly tear out.

5. Stick the dinosaur into the scene with glue.

What does a Triceratops use to do DIY?
A Dino-Saw

25

FOSSILS

Fossils are any animal and plant remains that are over 100,000 years old. They can be as small as shells and insects, or as big as giant dinosaurs. The word 'fossil' comes from the Latin word for 'dug up'. The most common fossil is Ammonite, often found on beaches all around the world.

1. Draw around a roll of sticky tape and cut the circle out.

YOU WILL NEED:
- CARD • SCISSORS • WHITE CRAFT GLUE
- DRIED PASTA • GREY PAINT • PAINTBRUSH

2. Spread a layer of glue over the card circle.

3. Use lots of different shapes of pasta to create a spiral.

5. Cover with a thin layer of white craft glue and leave to dry.

4. Paint the whole thing a dark grey colour and leave to dry.

VOLCANO

We don't know exactly why the dinosaurs became extinct 65 million years ago. Scientists believe it could be because a giant asteroid hit the Earth or perhaps a large volcano erupted that changed the Earth's climate so much that it was hard for any living thing to survive.

YOU WILL NEED:

- TWO PLASTIC CUPS • GLUE STICK
- STICKY TAPE • GREEN CARD
- BROWN/YELLOW/RED/ ORANGE PAPER
- SCISSORS

1. Cover one plastic cup with brown paper. Glue this on to some green card.

2. Cover another plastic cup in red paper.

3. Cut the top so that it is wavy and you can bend it over itself.

4. Add shorter layers of orange and yellow paper, with wavy edges over the red layer.

5. Stick this on to the top of the brown cup and secure in place by wrapping a strip of brown paper around the join.

WOOLLY BRACHIOSAURUS

The Brachiosaurus were sauropods, which means they had long necks and tails but small heads. They grew to be as tall as two double decker buses stacked on top of each other. Like giraffes, they fed from tall trees.

1. Cut into each end of one long cardboard tube.

YOU WILL NEED:
• 2 LONG CARDBOARD TUBES • 3 SHORT CARDBOARD TUBES • SCISSORS • GOOGLY EYES • WHITE CRAFT GLUE • WOOL • MASKING TAPE

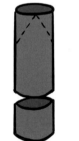

2. Make one of the short cardboard tubes smaller than the other, then cut triangles into the tops of each tube.

5. Cover with glue and start winding the wool around the tubes until it is all covered. Glue the googly eyes on to finish.

3. Cut the last short tube in half and then cut triangles into one end.

4. Stick the tubes together using the masking tape.

ICHTHYOSAURUS
PAPER SCULPTURE

YOU WILL NEED:
- LIGHT AND DARK BLUE PAPER • STICKY TAPE • SCISSORS • FELT-TIP PENS

The word 'Ichthyosaurus' is Greek for 'fish lizard' which suitably describes this species of reptile that once lived in the water. Unlike fish, they needed to breathe air. Their appearance was similar to a dolphin although they actually had more in common with land mammals.

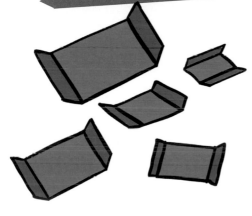

1. Cut out 5 rectangles, each one smaller than the one before. Fold each rectangle twice so that they look like they have 2 flaps.

2. Take the largest rectangle and tape this to the middle of a piece of paper.

3. Put tape on the other flap, bend into an arch and stick down. Repeat with all the other rectangles.

4. Cut out some fins and a tail and stick on to the rectangles.

5. Add an eye and mouth using a felt-tip pen.

AMBER INSECTS

Resin from trees is runny and sticky so it's easy for small animals and insects to get stuck. In the right conditions it will go hard and turn into amber meaning that it's possible to see things today that died millions of years ago, such as these Triassic mites.

YOU WILL NEED:

- BLACK PAPER • SCISSORS • PENCIL
- PERMANENT MARKER PEN
- WHITE CRAFT GLUE • YELLOW PAINT
- PAINTBRUSH • PLASTIC SANDWICH BAG
- GLUE STICK

1. Fold a piece of black paper in half and draw a circle shape on one side.

2. Use scissors to cut the circle out of both sheets of paper at the same time.

3. Mix the white craft glue with some yellow paint.

4. Draw the mite on one side of the plastic bag using the permanent marker pen and then paint the glue mixture on to the other side. Leave it to dry.

5. Glue the plastic in the middle of the two black sheets. Glue the black sheets to close.

DID YOU KNOW?
The oldest piece of amber that has been found is 320 million years old!

FLYING ICAROSAURUS

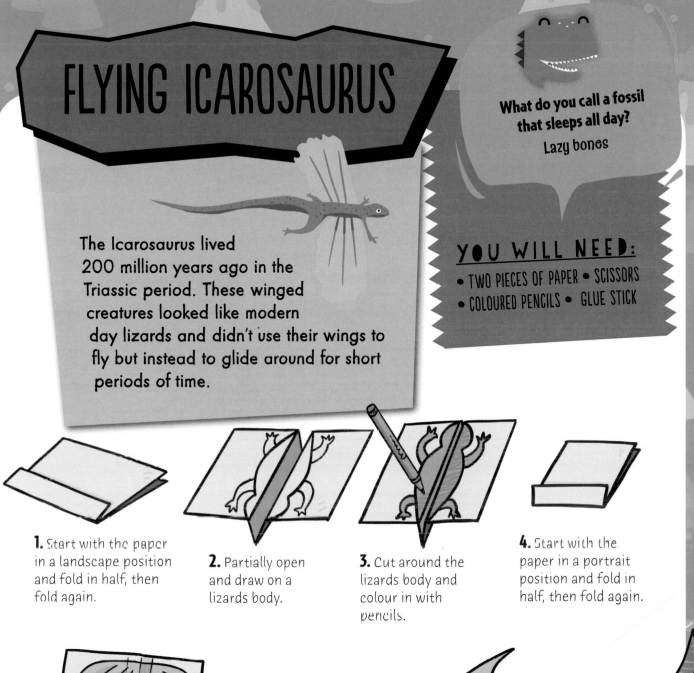

The Icarosaurus lived 200 million years ago in the Triassic period. These winged creatures looked like modern day lizards and didn't use their wings to fly but instead to glide around for short periods of time.

YOU WILL NEED:
- TWO PIECES OF PAPER • SCISSORS
- COLOURED PENCILS • GLUE STICK

1. Start with the paper in a landscape position and fold in half, then fold again.

2. Partially open and draw on a lizards body.

3. Cut around the lizards body and colour in with pencils.

4. Start with the paper in a portrait position and fold in half, then fold again.

5. This time open up and make the wings. Colour in before sticking on to the body.

6. Make a tail from some off cuts of paper and stick it to the body.

DINOSAUR PUZZLE

CAN YOU FIND THE ANSWERS TO THESE QUESTIONS?

1. How many palm trees can you spot?

2. Which of the lava trails reaches the T-Rex?

3. How many craters are there on the meteor?

4. Where is the second dinosaur hiding?

DISCOVER MORE...

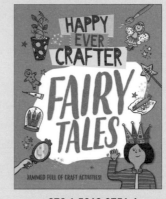

HAPPY EVER CRAFTER

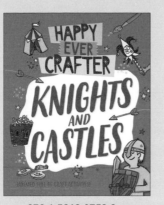

978 1 5263 0753 8

Realm of Knights and Castles
Kingdom of Costumes
King of the Castle
Invitations
Party Games
Party Decorations
Fantastic Feasts
Medieval Makes
Knights Puzzle

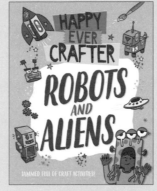

978 1 5263 0755 2

Sci-Fi Worlds
Outer Space Outfits
Planet Party
Intergalactic Invites
Party Games
Party Decorations
Space Food
Crafty Makes
Space Puzzle

978 1 5263 0751 4

Once Upon a Time
Costumes and Characters
Enchanted Accessories
Invitations
Party Games
Party Food
Party Decorations
Crafty Makes
Fairy Puzzle

978 1 5263 0713 2

Argh M' Hearties!
Daring Dressing Up
Pirate Plans
Invitations
Party Games
Party Decorations
Party Food
Crafty Makes
Pirate Puzzle

978 1 5263 0757 6

Dinosaur World
Big Beasts Fancy Dress
Prehistoric Party Plans
Invitations
Party Games
Party Decorations
Party Food
Craft-o-saurus
Dinosaur Puzzle

978 1 5263 0759 0

Amazing Animals
Cute Creature Costumes
Party Animal
Invitations
Party Games
In the Zoo
Tasty Treats
Creature Crafts
Animals Puzzle

WAYLAND

www.waylandbooks.co.uk

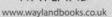